Pitching for Profit

The Bad Bitches' Playbook to
Convert Conversations
Into Currency

Precious L. Williams

Publishing Services By: Pen Legacy®
Cover By: Junnita Jackson
Editing & Formatting By: U Can Mark My Word Editorial Services

Library of Congress Cataloging – in- Publication Data has been applied for.

ISBN: 978-1-7366118-2-1

PRINTED IN THE UNITED STATES OF AMERICA

Table of Contents

Coming Back to Life
After Almost Giving Up

Pitching for Profit

The Bad Bitches' Playbook to
Convert Conversations
Into Currency

The Third Time Is a Charm

A s I pen this book, I can't stop reflecting on how the number three shows up in my life. For example, this will be my third published book. In prior pitch competitions, I was the 3rd contestant. I am the third individual to be named "Precious" in my family. I entered New York City on the 33rd PATH Train, and I was number 33 on my pledge line of the Eta Kappa chapter of Delta Sigma Theta Sorority, Inc. Most importantly, my grandmother, Precious D. Williams, was born in the year 1933. So, as you can see, the number three is significant to me.

With this third book, I plan to pour my growth and maturation into you—offering my playbook, processes, and profit-earning strategies I have mastered over the past ten years. It is my hope that by sharing my knowledge and experiences, you will be fully equipped and prepared to fight for your success like the true champ you are once you finish the final chapter.

This "ultimate pitch playbook" will educate you on leveraging every conversation by obtaining what you desire with precision. To ensure you fully receive the message, take a minute to think about and answer the following questions so you can pinpoint your strengths and weakness when it comes to your business, profession, or lifestyle.

➤ What do I need to elevate my business?
➤ Am I securing the number of clients I need daily to achieve my goal?
➤ Am I attracting the right media and press needed to propel my business in the right direction?
➤ Is my business in the right position to gain investors' interest in order to place my business next to multi-million-dollar brands?
➤ Am I gaining profitable referral partners, affiliates, and network connections that I can collaborate and learn from?

If you answered no to one or more of these questions, then you have found the right coach and picked up the right book. I will coach you by offering you tips, strategies, and the "how-to" when it comes to leveraging, positioning, and converting your conversations into powerful currency, not just money. However, only the unapologetic women who think outside the box and are comfortable marching to the beat of their own drum will benefit the most from my coaching. These types of women are not afraid to put in the work necessary to yield the desired results. My plan is to challenge you, remove you from every comfort zone, and help you see the potential you continue to run from or suppress.

I am honored you chose this publication to guide you as you embark on the next professional level of pitching and profiting.

Are you ready to dive in? Yes? Well, let's go!

Are You Ready to Maximize Your Profit?

Before we continue, let's define profit so that you are clear on the mission we are trying to achieve. According to Investopedia, profit is "the financial benefit realized when revenue generated from a business activity exceeds the expenses, costs, and taxes involved in sustaining the activity in question. Any profits earned funnel back to business owners, who choose to either pocket the cash or reinvest it back into the business. Profit is calculated as total revenue less total expenses."

Get it? Profit is the money you get to keep after paying your expenses. So, moving forward, we will focus on profits. Far too often, I hear entrepreneurs, business owners, and people in general celebrating revenue, which is not your business's wealth. Revenue is nothing more than the total amount of income generated by the sale of goods or services. Who doesn't get excited about making money? The key to leveraging your pitch is to offer a conversation that will increase your profit

Precious L. Williams

and, in return, build wealth.

Now that we are clear on our goal regarding profits, let's get back to business. To some of my clients, I am known as a poet and a rapper extraordinaire. Just kidding! However, one of my favorite songs is by Moneybagg Yo titled "Me vs. Me." My favorite verse in the song is *"**Going out the way I came!**"* This verse embodies my philosophy and mantra: "It is vital to understand the value in coming in with a vengeance and leaving a memory." When I enter any room, I walk in bold, powerful, confident, and very much in your face, unapologetically. I am not focused on making friends or snapping selfies for the 'Gram (Instagram). My goal is to slay and leave a long-lasting impression. I leave my imprint because who I am is everything you need, either in your life or business.

In my first book, *Bad Bitches and Power Pitches: For Women Entrepreneurs and Speakers Only*, I taught you the type of pitches every Bad Bitch needs in her arsenal. These pitches are based on the seven branding bitches we all have encountered in life or business. In the companion workbook, *Bad Bitches and Power Pitches*, I provided practical exercises and strategic assignments to help you get ready for the boardroom, stage, media, and investors by teaching you proven techniques that will create your industry domination. Now it's time to take things up a notch and learn how to convert your experience into currency while mastering profiting.

In this book, I will unveil how I learned how to use the power of pitching to add value to my business, brands, and books. Before, I was a speaker who embodied the eight attributes of a great speaker:

✓ Confidence
✓ Passion
✓ Be Yourself
✓ Voice Modulations

12

✓ Keep It Short and Sweet
✓ Connect with Your Audience
✓ Paint a Picture Through Storytelling
✓ Repetition

Today, I am a highly sought-after coach and pitch master employed by Microsoft, LinkedIn, Google, and NBC Universal. In addition, I work with Fortune 500 executives, speakers, and entrepreneurs. It has become my life's mission to help individuals pitch their way into media, multi-million dollar investments, higher employment positions, and to the bank. *Pitching for Profit: The Bad Bitches Playbook to Convert Conversations Into Currency* is written with a fresh perspective on accessing all types of currency simply by igniting your pitch, dominating your niche, and converting conversations into cash. Also, I provide you with practical hands-on tips that you can implement immediately.

By the time you have reached the end of this book, I hope you will have already started implementing the tools given and are now witnessing results. This is your playbook, so take the lessons and teachings and astronomically explode your business and lifestyle. As I coach you by way of these pages, I encourage you to take advantage of my twenty-six years of professional speaking experience. Having eleven years of experience as a successful serial entrepreneur, ten years of experience being the #KillerPitchMaster, and having accepted my honored role as the Ultimate Bad Bitch with a Power Pitch, I am excited about this opportunity to share my knowledge with you.

Are you ready to attract the tribe that fits your vibe? Are you ready to build your Bad Bitch Army? If so, let's go!

Never look back.
Never think twice.
Make a powerful decision, and let's make
"MONEY MOVES" like Cardi B!

The Winner's Mentality & Creed

What do winners do? We work hard, play hard, and get the job done. It's that simple! So that you get the most out of this book, let's set our winner's mentality and establish some rules of engagement.

> ➤ **WE ARE WINNERS AND ALL WE DO IS WIN.**
> We show up with a winner's mentality! Winners don't whine; we grind. We don't play; we slay. We make every play look effortless, yet we don't take the easy way out.

> ➤ **WE ALWAYS COME PREPARED THROUGH PRACTICE, PRACTICE, PRACTICE!**
> We pay close attention to our competitors to make the necessary adjustments to stay in the game. If we're going to play this game, we will make it hard for our opposition to see our next moves. Until you know who your top connections are and their resources, you are playing a

Precious L. Williams

losing game. So, let's do some accounting of what we already have and develop a plan to mobilize!

> **WINNERS THOROUGHLY RESEARCH AND STUDY THEIR COMPETITION.**
When was the last time you researched to see who your competition is, whether on Google or social media? Have you checked out your industry? Do you know what your competition is doing in the marketplace, and what makes them successful? Knowing these answers will help you build your branding, marketing, and advertising strategies, as well as when writing your pitch.

> **PAY ATTENTION TO THE TRENDS CURRENTLY HAPPENING IN YOUR INDUSTRY.**
To win BIG, pay close attention to what others are not seeing. What are the trends of other industries that you can bring into yours? Are you looking in trade journals? Are you looking at the state of your industry right now? Do you see some holes? Do you see some places that no one has taken advantage of yet? Start putting pen to paper, and let's get it poppin'!

> **FOCUS ON SETTING THE PERFECT FOUNDATION FOR YOUR BUSINESS AND SPEAKING CAREER BY TAKING A POWERFUL STANCE AGAINST THE ESTABLISHMENT.**
You are the only one who can see the flaws and loopholes in your competitor's arguments. Have a viewpoint that no one else is talking about. The reason you're taking an opposite position is because you want people to start focusing on you and the fresh perspective you bring to the marketplace.

16

➢ **BE CLEAR ON WHO YOUR TARGET MARKET IS AND HOW YOU CAN SERVE THEM BETTER.**
Your target market lies in defining specific sources where your products and services are most needed. It's almost like finding your low hanging fruit. Remember, your target market is a group of people toward which you have decided to aim your marketing efforts for maximum impact, exposure, and profits. Who should you be focusing on and why? I know every coach says you should focus on attracting people who have a high net worth and all that jazz. That's great. However, if you don't have your pitch together, you're not really in the game of attaining your most ideal clients.

As you see, conducting a competitive analysis is essential to any industry—whether sports, business, entertainment, or life. Some people think if you just start a business or publish a book, you're winning. I am here to debunk that myth. Having the ability to pitch, profit, and prosper requires strategy, planning, and research. Now that you have received my briefing, let's get to work.

Change Your Mindset,
Increase Your Profits

Knock *me down nine times, but I get up ten!* What a great verse from Cardi B's song, "Get Up 10." Let's examine this line a little more closely, shall we? In life, you will get knocked down, suffer defeat, and make a mess of situations you thought you could easily handle. No one makes it through this life unscathed. No one! However, you must keep getting up no matter what. Most people feel it is easier to stay down or hide in the shadows than face what comes with a renewed fire in your belly. Like you, I am ready to face today, tomorrow, and future days with zeal and enthusiasm. Think over your life. It has not been easy, but you also know ANY successful person—or hell, an UBER successful person—has had to fight against the odds to make it where they are today. Why? Because they refused to give up even though reaching success required possibly changing their original goal, being flexible in their execution, and building up their courage and resiliency muscles. What else did it require? For them to change their mindset!

Do you often play small because you cannot see the potential? Are you sitting on your gift because nobody has guaranteed you success in exchange for it? Are you taking the long way to reach your dreams because you are too afraid to go straight for them? Or have you given up because you feel you can't afford to pursue your dreams? That's the most common excuse I've heard. How long are you going to stand in the way of your money, lifestyle, growth, and legacy? Don't you realize that choosing to do nothing yields you nothing? Do you believe God blessed you with life only to stay in debt and leave this earth with unfulfilled dreams? Having this kind of mindset is why you are content with just working to get some money, but you need to understand that your revenue is only keeping you broke. If you want better than what you are presently offering yourself, you must change your perspective on your business, life, and professional goals. Trust me, it all comes down to making a decision and staying committed to it.

When pitching for profits, it's all about having a "take no prisoners" attitude. No longer should you feel the need to seek others' permission to be who you are and what you want to become. Our Father God has given you permission to become the entrepreneur or speaker you keep conversing about with your friends, family, co-workers, and on social media. That's the only one whose permission you need.

Aren't you tired of only talking about what it is that you want to do? Your success depends on being radical, unhinged, and a wild woman determined to gain what she knows she deserves. She exemplifies this quote: "Well behaved women seldom make history." Consider the fact that life truly begins once you step out of your comfort zone. You MUST be okay with not being okay and risking it all, leaving no other options on the table. The way I think is: "This has to work because I have no other choice." Thinking this way is how I stay committed to the process, brave enough to take the risk, and okay with being uncomfortable during the struggle to reach my success.

From this point forward, I challenge you to get uncomfortable, removing every safety net that makes these things easy to avoid. Between the job losses and unexpected deaths that occurred in 2020 as a result of COVID-19, don't you realize by now just how precious life is and why it's essential for you to stop putting off until tomorrow what you can do today? If you truly make the decision to succeed in business and life despite all odds, you WILL make it. Your conversations should start creating cash monthly or, better yet, daily. In addition to your conversations, your strategic relationships should contribute to leading you to enrich your life and the lives of others.

Now, many individuals sleep on their success because they're worried about haters and if their product, service, or speaking topic will be received or appreciated. Can I share another secret? It's good to have haters. If you have haters, you're doing something right. Haters should motivate you to excel, leaving them to bask in your wins. Whenever I achieve success, I make it my business to thank all of my haters for making me a fighter. It's impossible to stop a woman who can't quit! We are wired with stuff that others cannot see. They don't see the nails of determination, bolts of courage, wiring of commitment, and the staples of willingness. Be that woman who fights for your dreams, your money, and your relationships—the ultimate currency.

Lastly, please know it's okay to ask for the sale, for help, the opportunity, and a warm introduction to a connection. Stop thinking you have to create this big dream all by yourself. The more you ask now, the less asking you will have to do over time. That's why it's crucial that you make the concrete decision to go for it. Make your request so BIG, yet so strategic, that it becomes a win-win for both parties. However, always be prepared to reciprocate and be a helpful resource to

21

Precious L. Williams

others when asked. This can, on its own, open doors to hidden opportunities and networks.

COACHING CORNER:
SHOW UP LIKE YOU MEAN IT!

How are you showing up? It's time to bring forth your new mindset and attitude. Bring your 'A' game to the table and go out there like Muhammad Ali in his prime. Become the heavyweight champion in your world. How do you do that?

> **BE WILLING TO FIGHT FOR YOUR DREAMS!**
  Some of you haven't fought for your dreams because you never learned how to do so. You have found comfort in listening to people who lack your vision but offer their opinion. So, today, I want you to write out your dreams *(make it plain)* and be okay with trusting yourself to achieve them.

> **ASSESS WHAT YOU NEED INTERNALLY.**
  Is your spirit being nurtured? Do you need more confidence? What do you lack internally that is preventing you from succeeding? Write it down and look at it every day.

> **FACE THE IMPOSSIBLE AND DO THE DAMN THING ANYWAY!**
  Have you ever been told you weren't good enough, smart enough, talented enough, or pretty enough? If you answered yes to any of those, you are not alone. I'm raising my hand, too. Even though you were told that, do you believe it? Have you owned their views as your own? Let's be clear; you will always have individuals who are going to belittle, degrade, and

hinder your growth by speaking their fears into your being. Raise your self-esteem so you can face the impossible and win anyway.

➢ **CREATE AN IMAGE OF YOURSELF WINNING.** Live in your vision, not your reality. You are a conqueror and will make the impossible look easy. So, I challenge you to create a vision board and place a picture of yourself in the middle so you can see yourself achieving your goals. Go there before you get there.

➢ **WHO IS THE BURGER KING TO YOUR MCDONALD'S?** Who would you love to face off against? For me, my biggest naysayer has been my mother. I couldn't wait to say to her, "The child you gave away made it." The child she kicked to the curb outshined them all. Because of what I wanted to prove, I had to step my game up so my conversation would manifest. In addition to your naysayers, who is your competition? When you know who the Burger King is to your McDonald's, only then will you start operating in your zone of genius. Are you outshining your competition? Are you walking six steps ahead of them? Research and realign so you can sit at the table and kill it!

Pitching, Your Superpower

"**P**itching Is Bitching!" was the title of a *Forbes Magazine* article written about my first book, *Bad Bitches and Power Pitches*. Can I tell you how much I cried when Geri Stengel, a *Forbes* contributing writer, chose my book to write a controversial piece about? After receiving mixed messages regarding my title prior to the book's release, having a prominent magazine write this particular title and offer their review was breathtaking.

Let me remind you, at that point, I still considered myself to be that ugly black girl from St. Louis, Missouri, who no one wanted. In a sea of New York Times Bestsellers and books penned by more skilled writers and storytellers, my little book, based on my gift and love of pitching, was deemed newsworthy by a *Forbes* contributor—out of all the business media presses! In my opinion, *Forbes* is the absolute gold standard. How did it happen? Relationships, relationships, and more relationships! And yes, that one article turned my conversation into currency:

cash, opportunities, money, power, and respect!

As you can see, currency is not just about getting money. Currency, in this sense, is anything that creates opportunities that will yield multiple income streams and profitable income statements. When it comes to business, money is the reward. But it's what you do strategically to position yourself as the go-to expert that makes you worthy of a six-figure compensation just for you to show up. Currency is the tool needed to win, and hopefully, you are earning enough to have some left over. Remember, being profitable means being able to keep earnings after paying all your liabilities and expenses.

Building Currency Through Relationships

Never assume a person can't serve you because of where they are or where you're not in life. When it comes to building relationships, you never know who can help you or who GOD will put in your life to elevate you. My business connections are truly profitable because of my level of expertise, but trust me, it hasn't always been this way. In the beginning, I did not leverage the power of relationships. I was more fascinated with just being in the room and taking selfies to prove that I was in the presence of elite individuals. However, the sad truth is none of that mattered. The pictures with executives and celebrities did absolutely nothing for my career or name. Because they did not know me, they couldn't validate me, and I had no access to them. Does this sound familiar? Many people gain access to the right rooms but waste time focusing on going live to showcase and taking selfies for likes but leave the event the same way they entered—with nothing. As I learned by changing my network and mindset, the international speaker and serial entrepreneur leave every room with phone numbers, booked opportunities, and appointments for collaboration. I stopped taking selfies and worrying about proving anything to others who didn't know those people anyway. In fact, key holders can spot a groupie and will keep their distance from you. We are grown people making a living for our families, so it's always about business. But here is how I leveraged a relationship to gain my *Forbes* write-up.

I met the *Forbes* contributing writer through my relationship with working with Women Entrepreneurs NYC. This organization is a part of NYC Small Business Services, whose mission is to help women start, grow, and expand their businesses in New York and beyond. I went from attending events to becoming a WE/NYC mentor. I went from meeting the mentors and taking photos to becoming a highly sought-after coach that others eventually looked up to. See what you can become when you put the phone down and communicate!

Once I became serious about networking, WE/NYC featured me in *The Wall Street Journal*. Do you see the currency here? Having the relationship offered me press exposure, which in return afforded me sales, clients, and upped my value, especially financially. That's the cool thing about networking. People are always watching, and the people who see your potential will wait for you to stop playing and get serious about your business so they can open the doors to your success. Any event, speaking engagement, and training have the potential to turn your conversation into currency. Once you realize that, you will have a life that money can't buy.

Building Currency Through Pitching

The truth is pitching unlocks the doors that most cannot see. It is a known fact that messaging and connecting with audiences is a struggle for most women entrepreneurs and speakers. I am often surprised by how many of them don't invest in mastering their business communication. Don't you realize that the only thing standing in the way of your profit and luxury lifestyle is your ability to communicate? Then they wonder why they miss the most rewarding invitations and opportunities. I challenge you to claim your rightful place in herstory, invest in your pitching, and stop missing opportunities to network strategically. When you position yourself to win, the trade-off will be the currency needed to propel you.

Being a 13-time national elevator pitch champion, I know a thing or two about pitching. However, pitching is nothing if you don't know how to utilize your network, create strategic alliances, gain referrals and affiliates, and truly CRUSH your competition. When it comes to pitching for profits, you need to understand that you pitch every day of your life for attention, job promotions, recognition, speaking engagements, media interest, and maybe prize money. But what if I could share with you how you could pitch daily, get paid, and turn your small business into a global empire? Do I have your attention NOW?

If pitching is so powerful, why don't most individuals apply it to their business or career? As we grow in entrepreneurship and as speakers, very few are taught how to place a premium on how we break down the doors of adversity. Yes, we are told to have branding verbiage, killer graphics, or captivating marketing content on our website to resonate with prospects, yet very few ever learned how to utilize those things to create a pitch to close the deal. Pitching is a major part of securing clients, customers, and opportunities that we need to monetize our business. When it comes to pitching, you have to be able to open your third eye to read the room, understand group dynamics, and throw caution to the wind by being different on purpose. Doing these three things can save you and your business from utter failure.

As your coach, allow me to pour into your spirit that you DESERVE to be in any room that you desire. There is no SPACE you cannot occupy if you DARE. For some, pitching does not come naturally, as many people have trouble selling themselves. Just remember that your goal is to seize your moment through the power of communicating and capture everyone's attention, be it in written or verbal form.

When you think of pitching, remember this acronym...

- ➢ **P — Powerfully** presenting yourself, your business, and/or your speaking brand with supreme and utter confidence, daring others to look away.
- ➢ **I — Intentionally** seizing every moment to make a BIG impression. The name of the game is not to be liked but to be remembered and stand out. When someone is seeking your particular craft, you want to be the first person who comes to their mind.
- ➢ **T — Taking** advantage of every avenue to display your greatness and share your "secret sauce" that no one can EVER duplicate.
- ➢ **C — Captivating** and seizing others' attention in the first ten seconds of speaking or through written communication. Have them spellbound by your passion, energy, and intensity.
- ➢ **H — Having** the ability to close in a unique way, leaving no doubt that you are the #1 choice.

Now, can you see why "pitching is bitching" and, oh, so powerful?

COACHING CORNER:
THE POWER OF FOCUS

To win at this pitching game as a speaker and/or an entrepreneur, you need to be laser-focused. Why? Because being laser-focused wins games. Periodt! So, strap on your big girl panties because we are about to go in.

- ➢ **TO WIN AT A PROFESSIONAL LEVE' MUST BE AT A PROFESSIONAL**
  You must embody what your brand represent it to the fullest all day, ever

30

your marketing materials look like? Does your LinkedIn profile capture the true essence of what you can offer and have already done for others? How do you present yourself on social media? Do you exude professionalism, or do you come across as an amateur? WWE Wrestler and Hall of Famer Rick Flair said, "To be the best, you've got to beat the best!" And let me be really clear; this is not about spending a lot of money. It's about showing up as the professional you truly are.

➢ **NEVER LET THEM CATCH YOU SLIPPING.**
Remember, you set trends as well as the pace. That old Dodge commercial said it best: "You either lead, follow, or get out of the way!" Take this to heart!

➢ **LET YOUR PAST MISTAKES GO FOR GOOD.**
I know some of you may be thinking this is easier said than done. However, every time you take the field, it's a new game with new players. The past does not matter. Who you deal with today is the only thing that matters. Shake off all mistakes and see them as lessons. The game you played before, previous mistakes, and deals that didn't work out have absolutely nothing to do with who you're playing today. Every time you send out a proposal, pitch live, or conduct a sales call, don't think about what happened yesterday. All that matters is today and moving forward.

➢ **FOCUS ONLY ON WHAT YOU'RE GOING TO DO TODAY.**
Are you going to make five, ten, or one hundred sales calls? Do you plan to put together a list of your VIP and promising prospects so you can reach out to them? Will you go live on Facebook to connect with fans and gain new supporters? If so, what will you choose as a topic?

I need you to set the plan for your day. This day is not like yesterday, and it won't be like tomorrow. What are you going to focus on today? Jot it down on paper or put it in your calendar. Then do it!

> **FOCUS ON WHERE YOU WANT TO BE AND MAKE MOVES TOWARDS THIS VISION.**
Live in your vision, not your reality. There are going to be a lot of distractions that are going to try to get in your way. There will be a lot of people talking in your ear. It's going to be a lot of things making you doubt yourself. But, as I said before, I need you to focus on what you can take action on right now. That means changing your attitude to that of a winner. That means walking in with confidence and focus to the exclusion of everything else.

> **BE RUTHLESS.** What do I mean by being ruthless? I mean, you need to let go of those people who add little purpose to your life. We all have those friends, family, and so-called loved ones who try to hold us back. Learn to let them go and move on in the spirit of love and peace. You cannot serve two masters. You have GOD, who directs and runs the plays with you and gives you the vision to keep it going. Surround yourself with winners—people in your network who are grinding and showing you that you can do it. They have made it and are making it. They have a positive attitude. Even when they have bad days, they still consider themselves blessed because they know tomorrow is a new day.

> **BE RELENTLESS.**
Did you know that persistence beats resistance all the time? You may hear no's now, but when we take that field, all I want you to hear in your mind is, "They're

31

going to say yes!" Every time you lace up your boots, it's on. Whenever you put on your gear, don your armor, and gather your arsenal, be relentless. Don't stop! Don't quit! Why is that? Because the race is not won by those who are fast or have great strength but by those who do not quit.

Igniting Your Pitch

Have you ever heard the song "Fuckin' Problems" by A$AP Rocky? It starts with the line "I love bad bitches, that's my fuckin' problem," and this chorus is repeated three times. I can relate because the truth is, I love bad bitches, too. In my opinion, too many women are playing small and turning that bullshit into an art form! And when I say I love bad bitches, I'm referring to those women who know who she is, are comfortable in her skin, and is about her business daily. No apologies given. That's my kind of woman! Is that you? If so, we need to connect so I can help you ignite your pitch and take over your industry with excellence.

Igniting your pitch is about grabbing your audience's attention quickly and with precision. Now, let me warn you, this is not an easy job by any means. It requires staying focused, paying attention to wordplay, and being fearless enough to try and try again. When I first established Perfect Pitches by Precious, LLC, I was grateful for anyone who became my client. Is that where you are right now? I had no specific niche, and it showed in the quality and quantity of my clients. They ran the gamut because I ran the gamut. I didn't do the necessary work to zero in on my target market, resulting in many hits and just as many misses. As I look back, my lack of preparation, planning, and research held me back from reaching my fullest potential until late 2018, early 2019. With no real strategy, I became irritated with coaching because I could not measure who was my ideal client.

However, when I became clear on my ideal client, highly professional, successful women aspiring to embark on a new journey began hiring me. They needed my guidance to motivate them to go after their business and/or speaker dreams. They mainly fell between the ages of 35-59 and had major life experiences that shaped their mindset of wanting more but feared stepping out of their comfort zone. Today, I work with women of all ages who are so uncomfortable that they are eager to make that BIG investment in me!

When it comes to igniting your pitch, answer these questions: *What is it about your business, book, product, or service that lights your soul on fire? Is it your first potential sale? Is it making a difference in the lives of others and having a positive impact? Are you being paid handsomely for the vision you executed?* Living in these experiences will help you ignite your "why" and the enthusiasm to convey why you are the leading expert in your field. When you ignite your pitch, that's when you make money while you sleep. The business begins to sell itself, and you receive the ability to live life more.

Be it an elevator, media, investor, speaker, or interview pitch, always remember that igniting your pitch begins in your mind. What are you telling yourself daily? What loving, kind, and positive affirmation diet are you steadily feeding your mind? For me, these are my daily affirmations:

- I am the G.O.A.T. — Greatest of All Time.
- My doubters will become my believers! Trust that!
- My past is history, my present is a gift, and my future is limitless.
- I was born to conquer any and all situations.
- I stand before GOD, who built me to make the impossible look easy!
- I stay ready.
- I am thirsty on the grind.
- I cannot be stopped.
- I know my purpose and will work to achieve it every day.
- Nothing can stop me; I'm all the way up! (Fat Joe, Remy Ma)
- I am not new to this; I am true to this. (Little James)
- If you thought you've seen it all, the BEST is yet to come!
- GOD woke me up this morning. Time to make my dreams happen.
- Nothing and no one can take away my destiny BUT me!
- I trust myself completely to have my back.
- I stay in the land of positivity and abundance.
- As haters do their job, I will stay doing mine.
- Let's conquer this day! NOW!

How did saying those affirmations make you feel? You are what you speak into your existence. You are what you believe you are. Your true strength lies in focusing on the things you do well, not on the things you cannot change. From this day forward, feed yourself a daily diet of positive affirmations, despite what the world says about you. Affirming and manifesting is critical to assure you access all types of currency through the power of pitching simply because it gives you the passion, energy, and intensity to bring your "A" game. So, are you ready to **Ignite Your Pitch**?

Precious L. Williams

First, it requires you to see your business and career as the ultimate Super Bowl, World Series, NBA Finals, The World Cup, The Olympics, etc. What are your ultimate goals? To win, right? To ignite your pitch, let's examine your strategy. It all comes down to this:

- ➢ Are your communication skills top-notch?
- ➢ What is your strategic plan of attack?
- ➢ Are you in position to close the deal with your messaging, content, and sales pitch?
- ➢ Are you thoroughly prepared to pitch like your life depends on it?

Here are a few things to have clarity about as you get ready to kick ass. Commit to the following RIGHT NOW!

- ➢ *Commit to the #150Challenge!*
  Before meeting with a qualified prospect, company, foundation, non-profit, college, university, etc., put together a list of 150 reasons why they should hire you, promote you, or give you a shot. Be prepared to answer the silent questions and objections with cold hard facts, statistics, and social proof. Put them at ease from the very beginning. When igniting your pitch, the buck starts here!

- ➢ *Commit to the #365VisibilityChallenge!*
  Did you know that visibility trumps ability? *(Dr. Cheryl Wood)* When people see you featured everywhere, they naturally begin to get curious about you. *What is so special about her? What is up with all the hype?* Curiosity often turns prospects into new clients, customers, fans, and followers and helps build a network that you can monetize.

36

So, what exactly is the #365VisibilityChallenge? This challenge requires you to make a yearlong commitment to do something on social media daily—from podcasting to writing blogs, to LinkedIn and Facebook Lives, creating videos, etc. You want your audience to experience the real you, not the perfect "made for TV" you often presented to others. Russell Brunson taught this in his *One Funnel Away Challenge*. After I started teaching live on Facebook, my sales increased by 150% on my books. I also received more client inquiries, booked more lucrative speaking gigs, and gained more VIP clients. I have NEVER been this busy and HAPPY in my life!

You may be asking yourself, *Why is ALL this important to my entrepreneurial business pursuits or pitching?* Well, it's important because it creates that human factor that makes others see themselves in you. People tend to see your success and believe you don't have everyday "life problems." I don't know why we dehumanize people once they appear to be successful. Success has never stopped life, and for many, life hits harder the more successful you become. People need to see that, and you need to be ignited on your messaging, content, and pitch. When you speak, you are pitching—even if it's about you. You are selling yourself daily. When people see you as a real human being, no matter your success level, they come back repeatedly because you are giving them relatable information and results from betting on you. This #365VisibilityChallenge builds up your authentic voice, which in turn will build a following that will show support by purchasing your products and services.

LinkedIn picked me as a content creator because they saw I was organically building a following with real, concrete, transparent content. I do not feel the need to be perfect or always have the best outfit and makeup. The truth is, as entrepreneurs and speakers, our journey is not perfect, and it's okay to show your audience that. Use social media daily for one year, and you will see how much it will level up your business, drive traffic to your website, and position you as a new shero in your industry. Now that you understand the #365VisibilityChallenge, let's dive into some of the pitching assumptions hindering you from igniting your pitch and mastering how to pitch for profits.

First, let me address the biggest assumption of them all. Just because you attended some classes, seminars, or conferences, that does not make you a pitch master. I mean, think about it. How many classes, seminars, or conferences have you attended, and how does your bank account look right now? Is your bank balance escalating from new clients, or are you still depending on that paycheck from your employer? Are you hustling for that sale, or are you enjoying life as your service sells itself? If your business is stagnated or not bringing in enough earnings, here are some pitching secrets.

> **YOU ARE NOT PITCHING ENOUGH.**
  Every day you should be pitching yourself, whether on social media, via email, LinkedIn, etc. The more you do this, the more familiar people become with you. When I refer to pitching, I mean personalizing it for a particular person or group. We all hate canned pitches, especially the ones that have nothing to do with us. Take the time to study up on those you want to approach and start a real conversation. The conversation will then lead to pitching. The more you do this, making relationships your priority, you will begin to see how to tweak your pitch to attract more. Remember, one-and-done pitching is a thing of the past.

> **YOU ARE PITCHING TO THE WRONG AUDIENCE.**
  Trust me when I say we have all been there. We keep pitching to people who cannot afford us or do not see

our value. So, what do we do? Have a trusted business associate look at your web copy, pitch, and other materials to see where the disconnect is. Are you clear on your target market? One way to find out is to test your pitch on different audiences and networking groups. Ask their opinions. Typically, when you genuinely ask others to help, they will. This saves you time, missed opportunities, and it may even net you new clients or offer you a new approach that will make you the #1 choice in another market.

> **YOUR PITCHES ARE NOT GOOD ENOUGH.**
You read how to create a pitch and repeatedly try to make it work, but it still ends up sounding bland and generic. Again, ask your trusted advisors to provide honest feedback on how they see you versus what you present in your pitches. Are they moved to work with you? Why or why not? Get input and go back to the drawing board. Here are some key questions to consider: Are you addressing real pain points? What specific problem do you solve? What makes your solution different? Are you competing on value or price? Seeking low-hanging fruit or VIPS? Short or long sales cycles?

> **YOU ARE NOT "STARTING OFF WITH A BANG AND ENDING WITH FIREWORKS!" (Dr. Cheryl Wood)**
Similar to being boring, you are not making it clear that your products and services are the best. You sound like everyone else by stating your name, your company's name, and using generic language. Just fucking stand out! Ask a startling question, drop a groundbreaking statistic, or even take a dramatic pause. You should want all eyes on you. Give them a show and show the

fuck out! Challenge their assumptions and give them something to think about. The choice is yours. Make it count. The beginning sentence should set it off, and the closing should leave them breathless. Get to it!

> **YOU DON'T HAVE ENOUGH PITCHES IN YOUR ARSENAL FOR THE DIFFERENT AUDIENCES YOU MAY ENCOUNTER.**
> Recycling the same pitch on different audiences never works. Try changing things around to fit the needs of specific audiences. How you speak to finance professionals is different from how you would communicate with creatives, especially if you have products and services that serve them both. Again, ask yourself the previously mentioned questions and craft different pitches to satisfy different audiences. Then start the rotation.

Do any of these pitching pointers sound familiar to you? Better yet, have any of them even crossed your mind? It's time to stop passively pitching and get serious. Remember, your pitch defines your profit! Are you hungry enough to win?

COACHING CORNER:
THE POWER OF COMMITMENT

When it comes to pitching, you need to be committed to doing something daily that scares the hell out of you. Here are some of the things I want you to commit to this week:

> Call a friend and ask if they can warmly introduce you to someone you would love to connect with for your business and/or speaking career.
> Post a controversial question on social media and

DARE to have a REAL opinion on it. It will inspire your audience to respond and create dialogue. It may even gain media attention!

➤ Contact organizations, non-profits, and foundations. Offer to speak for FREE to their staff and even their clients on a timely and relevant subject. Once you get in and wow them, build the relationship and start pitching for more.

➤ Reach out to podcasts and guest bloggers. You will reach more people who never knew you before and increase your followers.

➤ Address your origin story. Create a video or audio and share with others how you began as an entrepreneur and speaker. Relate the good, the bad, and the ugly. Share your make-or-break moments, build suspense, and express why you are still at it today.

➤ Commit to utilizing, mobilizing, and monetizing your network! Yes, I said what I said! Remember, you cannot successfully build your enterprise alone. You need testimonials, referrals, and affiliates. All of these can help you in ways you can't imagine right now. How? The more people you deliberately engage with and ask for opportunities, the faster, bigger, and stronger you will grow.

➤ Commit to reaching out to about one to five VIPS! Don't wait for them to acknowledge you, because that might never happen. Like you, they are busy, too. So, make sure to have your pitches ready before you interrupt them from whatever they were doing before you contacted them. Also, and this is very important...build the relationship first. Research them before reaching out to them. Do something that will grab their interest and never let go.

Years ago, while in college, I wanted to become a Delta

Sigma Theta Sorority, Inc. member so bad I could taste it. Despite not knowing what a sorority was or who they considered an ideal candidate, I knew I had to stand out. Every chance I got, I would let them know who I was, how thorough I was, and how I would be a good selection. I even started exhibiting slight stalker-like behavior, sending every member in the chapter a weekly personalized email to share what I had learned about each of them. I left no stone unturned! I cannot tell you how it thrilled me to write over thirty emails each week, showing my eagerness for what I had learned about them. Like clockwork, I sent the emails, and I knew they looked forward to reading them. In addition to sending emails, I always showed up to their events two to three hours early.

Was it necessary? No! But, to me, I was willing to do whatever it took to obtain membership. My efforts proved to them that I was not playing. At that time, they were my VIP's, and I didn't hesitate to let them know that. I did not care if I appeared stupid or pressed. My goal was to make the line and prove to myself that I could do it. Even though many told me that my dedication was a bit much, I did not care! It should also be noted that I already had excellent grades, was a leader in various school positions, and had already been accepted into top law schools. To me, this opportunity would be the cherry on top.

And guess what? After all of that, I was selected! I made the line! I am proud to say my hard work paid off. The lesson here is: Go the extra mile to get noticed. More than likely, they are going to talk about you anyway. So, give them a show! I made it into the hardest sorority on Spelman College's campus. I am 33HK01, "Blood Sweat and Tears," and I am proud of it. When I made the line, many women walked up to me and told me that because I made it, they believed they could, too. They had been discouraged because of their backgrounds or thought no one would look at them. I made history to them, and I did it the right way—by displaying my talent, strength, determination, and never giving up! Who are your VIPS? How will you reach them? What are you willing to do to stand out?

Convert Your Pitch into Ultimate Profit

Let me just say, your "ultimate profit" begins and ends with you. Can pitches make you rich and ultimately wealthy? Better yet, can your pitch lead to your ultimate profit goals? Hell yes! As I have stated before, pitching is an essential component of your sales and marketing strategy. However, you must understand this is something you can't do on your own. A team is needed to break out of your local tribe and into the big leagues. Building a team/tribe locally, regionally, and nationally will increase and expand your ability to pitch based on their exposure, conversations, and new introductions.

If you have read my other books, you know your "pitch bitch" type. This is both important and necessary. By knowing your business (bitching) style, you will know what pitches will resonate with your audience, how to write them, and perfect the art of storytelling. When it comes to pitching, having a clear understanding of yourself is vital as it plays a big part in your branding. If you have not read *Bad Bitches and Power Pitches: For Women Entrepreneurs and Speakers Only*, stop reading now, read that book, and then come back and finish reading this one. Pitching and branding are in sync and can only deliver when you've mastered the other.

Now that you know who you are as a brand, have you created one or a few pitches? How do you feel about them? Are they converting? If yes, great! If not, it's time to start engaging and implementing what I have shared thus far in this book.

Another way to gain exposure is by getting your network to engage with others on your behalf. I would always hear people say, "It's not what you say that attracts; it's what others say about their experience with you that matters." Word of mouth sets the tone and reputation of how you will be perceived in these streets. Have you ever purchased something because a trusted friend, family, celebrity, or influencer encouraged you to buy it? Word-of-mouth marketing is pitching that can yield profits if done right.

You might be asking yourself, *How does pitching lead to profiting?* Strategic pitches produce all types of currency that you can trade in.

COACHING CORNER: REAL CURRENCY MOVES

Affiliates

Do you sell a product, service, or book? Are you getting the sales you would like it to at this point? Probably not! This is where affiliates come in. Affiliates are people who actively promote your products, services, and books to their unique networks in exchange for a cut or percentage of the total sales. They are usually given a custom link to track their sales and know how much monetary compensation they should receive monthly in exchange for ACTIVELY promoting what you are doing. It also works for events, seminars, conferences, etc. Sometimes affiliates go by other names, such as ambassadors. It pays to have a select group of affiliates working for your business because having them introduce your products, services, books, etc., to other people's market is worth its weight in gold.

Referrals

I love referrals because, most times, they are unexpected. As a member of 3-4 powerful networking groups, I know that referrals can be critical to your business's survival. It is also a form of word-of-mouth marketing/advertising. In many of my groups, referrals are appreciated but not mandatory, making it so much sweeter when a referral partner encourages someone to work with you. One week alone, three people told their friends about my services, and they booked me for pitching services. I was so surprised! Not only did I thank them profusely, but I also gave them a referral fee that they were NOT expecting. This encouraged them to reach out to more people because they had no clue I rewarded monetarily and with brownies!

Networking

Are you utilizing your network effectively? Are you turning your trusted networking partners into cash cows for your business, brand, and speaking career? If not, let me impress upon you that you are networking all wrong. Networking is about starting and maintaining relationships with others who can become referrals, affiliate partners, and even clients. Most of the time, it takes time. Just like you, I don't recommend anyone until I have developed an attachment for them, seen them demonstrate their zone of genius, or have personally worked with them. Again, this takes time, but it's worth it. Now, I'm not saying that you attend every networking

Precious L. Williams

event, be it virtual or physical. I would suggest selecting 1-3 networking groups and then see what feels right to you. What does a networking group emphasize? Relationships, fun while learning more about members, training and instruction, bonding, etc. These all make a BIG difference. When selecting your networking groups, remember to:

➢ **BE CONSISTENT IN YOUR ATTENDANCE** — Your fellow members/attendees will want to get to know you if they feel they can count on you to be there. So, show up and show out!

➢ **PARTICIPATE IN 1 ON 1'S** — What do I mean? Take advantage of having private one-on-one meetings with members Get to know them. Have an agenda that is not so business heavy. Spend time having real conversations and see where it takes you. You may find a real friend, referral partner, affiliate, and MAJOR supporter.

➢ **CELEBRATE YOUR WINS AND THE WINS OF OTHERS** — Reach out to others when they are in their winning season. Send them a card, make a BombBomb.com video specifically for them, shout them out on social media, buy their book, and put them on blast just because you can. It means a lot to your network that they can count on you when times are good and with you seeking ABSOLUTELY nothing in return!

Social Proof

This alone is one of the greatest ways to stand out in a crowded marketplace and make a BIG impact on your bottom line. Social proof is reflected in your RESULTS for your clients and customers. Their testimonials on working with you (especially on LinkedIn and other social media sites), media and press coverage, and even where you have already spoken or will be speaking in the future holds a lot of weight. As a speaker for twenty-six years, when people see Microsoft, LinkedIn, and Google listed as my clients, they are stunned that a curvy, highly-educated black woman like myself keeps getting into the supposed "ivory tower" without having an Ivy League degree. The fact that I have the REAL relationships that I have developed in media, financial, real estate, coaching and consulting, investors, etc., truly blows my prospects' minds!

Visibility

Visibility within your network and to your referral and affiliate partners is critical. That is why it's important to keep them abreast of updates on you every 1-3 months. One way to do this is via email. As you progress as an entrepreneur and speaker, remember not everyone sees all your posts on social media. So, take it upon yourself to keep your network in the know about current and past happenings since you last engaged them. Your forward momentum will inspire them and keep you top of mind with them. I still send my VIPs and business associates updates every 1-3 months, depending on how much is going on with my brand and me. What goes into these emails?

> ➤ I thank them for supporting me on my business and life journey.
> ➤ I discuss my wins and upcoming speaking gigs (BIG and small).
> ➤ I speak about awards I have won and include pictures from the award ceremonies that they may or may not have attended.
> ➤ I share pics and celebratory emails regarding the awards I have received for my books.
> ➤ I let them know if I have any BIG Asks they can assist me with, such as warm introductions, upcoming speaking

gigs, and connections that I need their help establishing.

➤ I thank them for taking the time to read my emails.

What are the results of doing this? I have had television appearances, media shout-outs, an increase in book sales, and PAID speaking gigs. Television networks have even approached me for possible shows built around my brand and me! Each of these will skyrocket your visibility, gain your business new clients and customers, and ultimately rock your bank account! Which of these currency moves will you commit to doing for the next 1-3 months?

Dominate Your Niche Through Pitching

I don't know about you, but I have no desire to be average, random, or ordinary. It's not my style at all! But most people, even women, have a strong need to fit in with their peers. To be taken seriously, you have to rise above the masses, not just regurgitate popular so-called gurus and coaches. You have to take your craft and industry by storm.

For some of you, this is going to be hard to do. You might feel there is safety in numbers and want to be popular. Let me be clear. Being popular doesn't always lead to you getting paid. The truth is, you want to make a real difference, have a big impact, and make cold, hard cash. Better yet, you want results. Well, let me tell you now, you are going to piss people off as you pass them by during your climb to greater success. I bet you didn't know familiarity breeds contempt. Some people want you to fly but not higher than them. It's cool for you to set goals, but your dear friends may become enemies when they see you achieving your goals through strategic and cunning pitching. Pay them no mind; you have a mission and a vision to focus on achieving. The people at the top are ready to welcome you, especially when they see you are not led or easily swayed by what others think and do. To reach the top and be a titan of your industry, you have to be all in and let the chips fall where they may!

How do you do that? How do you stand out in a sea of vanilla? You do it by pitching differently and staying focused on the goal at hand. By being focused on #creatingyourownlane. Even if you are a motivational, transformational, inspirational, educational, or entertaining speaker, you MUST carve out your own niche within your industry. Have you noticed that many have taglines after their names? It's because they are looking for any way to differentiate themselves and attract certain speaking opportunities. Yes, my speakers, you can attract speaking gigs that have not even made it to the market yet! Keep reading to see how.

In every industry or profession, you have those at the top who are the dreaded gatekeepers. Want to know how I feel about them? FUCK a gatekeeper! Their role is to keep the undesirables and other riffraff out, but I try not to acknowledge them. They have a job to do, and so do I. In any profession, the top people are chosen to be the face of these professions and the standard-bearers. Just like you, if we are keeping it a whole buck, I have been in many situations where the gatekeepers have blocked me from the top leaders. Why? Because I did not fit the mold of what they were expecting. Maybe it was my race, gender, or class. Perhaps my very presence was threatening to them. Yet, I paid them no mind and just kept being persistent. As you know, persistence beats resistance ALWAYS! I was not what they wanted, nor were they willing to give me a chance. At first, it hurt my feelings and made me angry. Now I know they did me a favor! Their keeping me out with their fake, plastic smiles caused me to be hungrier and grittier, which resulted in me beating them at their own game.

They made me a fighter who played to win. They REFUSED to see my greatness. What a gift! A true and utter gift!

Because I was not part of the in-crowd, it forced me to see the speaking world and the entrepreneurial world differently from others. I no longer listened to gurus who made breaking into the profession sound so easy. Maybe if I were a different race and gender, perhaps, but that was and is not my lot in life. If I couldn't join them, then I would beat them by sheer force of will.

How did I do it? Through the power of creating and owning my niche: pitching, public/professional speaking, and my unique approach to the communication arts space as a world-class communicator. I became the #KillerPitchMaster who specializes in all things pitching. Who was my competition? Hardly anyone. Now I do not have to compete for speaking engagements with motivational, transformational, or inspirational speakers. Business started coming to me because I create my own niche, ahem, lane.

Where do *you* start? Start by looking at your unique gifts, abilities, strengths, and talents. Were you content with playing small in someone else's sandbox? Or do you know you are destined for more? Were you defining yourself as the industry currently sees you? Or is your vision much BIGGER than your current reality? Just like you, I am used to being underestimated. It's still a fun game to play! As you know, we play to win as Bad Bitches. So, let's play the game, as the narrator says in the movie *Saw*.

Break the mold. Break what you do as entrepreneurs and speakers down into its base elements. As you do this, you will start to see your niche very clearly.

As a speaker, what do you usually address in your speeches and presentations? Better yet, what audience would you most want to speak to? I know some of you are going to say your ideal audience is wealthy, affluent, high-paying clients. Realistically, are you there yet to attract them? Have you paid your dues and perfected your craft? Have you targeted those who need you most and can afford to pay you? Do you have different pay scales and tiered options for various markets? This is critical so that many can work with you to learn your talents, skillsets, and abilities, thus growing as coaches with you as your brand grows and develops.

Since we are asking real, hard-hitting questions, what trending topics light your soul on fire? What could you speak about at length at any given time, no problem? What topic subjects are truly your jam?

Start there! Then break it down even further. Why? Because you are now creating multiple speaking topics, engagement ideas, and even books based on your answers to these questions. You are also getting clearer on your zone of genius. Take these questions seriously, my Bad Bitches. You are setting yourself up to go straight to the top of your industry and profession. Is this going to be easy? No! Will it be worth it? Check your bank account now. Note what is in there. Then check back in a few months and ask yourself that same question after seeing how your paper is stacked and how your confidence has grown!

COACHING CORNER:
HOW TO SLAY ALL DAY

Now, a little more on turning your conversations into currency. The HARDER you go creating your own lane and niche and remaining visible on social media will allow more opportunities in your life. But it starts somewhere. Here we go!

IF CONTENT IS KING, IS THE CONTENT YOU ARE PUTTING OUT WORTHY OF THAT TITLE?
Are you regurgitating what some coach has already taught you? Have you synthesized it and made it your own? I eat,

sleep, and breathe pitching. At least six days a week, I am working on my clients' pitches, creating cool PowerPoint presentations for corporate and nonprofit clients, etc. It brings me nothing but joy. I also write poetry and recite them on my Facebook Lives, getting rave reviews. I post 4-6 times daily on social media. Is it overkill, or am I doing things no one else is doing? You be the judge. Does it get my clients and me RESULTS? Hell yes! What are you willing to do to stand out and be different? Are you willing to be talked about in a good or bad way? I am!

KNOW WHO AND WHAT TO CHARGE FOR YOUR EXPERTISE.

One of the things I see many speakers and entrepreneurs struggle with is what to charge for their expertise. Now, I'm going to go against the grain and admit that I feel a lot of new speakers have no business charging because they don't even have a grasp on their craft. They aren't working with a coach and have no idea what to do. So, they sink and ultimately fail. That is why having a trusted network and utilizing their dopeness and resources is vital. When I changed my network to where I was not the bright light but instead learning how to start flickering, it changed my life. I learned to ask for help from others. I learned that having a tribe and a team is worth it while growing as a speaker and serial entrepreneur. From my 3-4 main networks, I learned to scale to new heights and price accordingly. What a relief it was when I brought in two different business coaches and changed my network. Since they had been in my shoes before and I had never been in theirs, it made all the difference!

THE IMPOSTER SYNDROME — WHO DO YOU THINK YOU ARE?

I'm a Bad Bitch with a Power Pitch. That's who, MF'er! *Am I good enough? Can I truly stand with the greats?* Every last entrepreneur and speaker has encountered these feelings of doubt. I challenge you to think so highly of yourself that it hurts! Why? Because it's not your lack that scares you. It's the fact that you got in the room despite your flaws. Your light frightens you. If you can do this and make the impossible look easy, what else can you do? I believe most people struggle with success. Success, not failure, is the real fear. When you are successful, everyone wants a piece of you. So, you tell yourself that fearing failure is safer to your heart, mind, and soul than acknowledging that success begets greater success. Are you willing to put in everything to make it? That's the real tea! Are you willing to put your killer pitches to the test daily? Are you willing not to get distracted? Let's get it popping!

HOW ARE YOU PRESENTING YOURSELF PUBLICLY?

What can people expect when you #rocthemic or bless the microphone? Are they able to learn more about you as well as your craft? Are you doing Facebook Lives and even taking questions? We often think our hard work will be enough, but it's not if no one shouts you out, recommends you, or sends you testimonials that you can use to attract more business opportunities.

DO YOU LEAD WITH YOUR TAGLINE OR WHAT DO YOU WANT TO BE KNOWN FOR?

Your tagline should always be one of the first things you lead with so that people associate it with you and only you. Gone are the days where merely saying your name is enough, and this is coming from a woman with a unique name. So, trust me on this.

It's Showtime

You all know how much I love truth bombs! Especially the types that say so little yet say the MOST! While going through this book, you have learned about baiting, attracting, and sealing deals through the power of strategic conversation. Would you like to be let in on another truth bomb that will blow your mind? Even if you have heard it before, it may hit you a bit differently when explained more fully.

The secret to staying #bookedandbusy with new clients, speaking engagements, media, and investors is to **leave them always wanting more**. Keep your energy up throughout your content, presentations, pitches, and conversations. Then watch the money roll in. Right now, you may be saying to yourselves, *I already do that!* I beg to differ.

In this new day and age, we live in a virtual world. There was once a time people networked immediately after pitching or being a speaker at an event. Nowadays, you have to wait for follow-up emails and phone calls. After every speaking event, the hosts or some heavy hitters that were in the room reach out to tell me that, at first, they thought my segment would be boring, but it actually sparked something in them and changed their perspective regarding communication and business pitching. The material I create and teach is memorable because my energetic personality gives it life! I approach every speaking engagement as a performance. In my mind, I am putting on a show. I am entertaining, educating, and engaging with people while leaving my imprint on them, which usually results in them booking me for their event. Dr. Cheryl Wood refers to it as "starting off with a bang and ending with fireworks!" So now I have to ask you, what is your performance strategy? Are you only giving them a conversation, or are you a showstopper for the ages? A delight? A spectacle? Are your speaking topics worthy of Broadway!

I am here to debunk another myth: your credentials, educational background, and contacts are not enough to land that contract or cash in on that six-figure client. People no longer care about your formal education and skillset. They are concerned with your results, your access, and the guarantee you can offer them. You never know who is in the audience. You never know who will be that change agent in your life. Do you always know who is watching and waiting to speak to you? That is why it's important to give the performance of a lifetime that offers promises and guarantees. That requires experience, not education.

My experience is what separates me from many of my competitors. My speaking topics are given through experience, not based on the textbook information I learned at Spelman. Every time I enter a room with others, be it virtually or physically, it's showtime! I come taking nothing for granted and ready to claim all opportunities. To some, I am a bit extra, but I'm a PAID extra. To others, I am a captivating and thrilling ride! That's why your pitch always needs to be polished, conversational, fresh, impactful, and, dare I say, dramatic. What's the point in pitching if it will not be memorable?

So how do you do this? I know. I know. I have some introverts who are reading this book and ready to give up right now. Please don't. As introverts, you offer your unique flavor to the equation. Like extroverts, you also need to gain new clients, customers, and attain business. You cannot do that sitting on the sidelines. So, I am asking you to trust me and play to your strengths. In my last book, I discussed learning the foundations of a basic pitch, which is still very important. In your basic pitch, you are answering the following questions:

➤ Who are you?
➤ What do you do?
➤ Who do you primarily serve? Who is your target audience?
➤ What makes you different? Why should someone choose you to work with over others?
➤ How do you do it?
➤ What are the next steps potential clients should take to work with you?
➤ Powerful call to action. (Say what you want them to do to express an interest in working with you. Instruct them to contact you to book an appointment, visit your website, check out your products and/or services, etc.)

Before moving forward, my question to you is, while reading this book, have you considered changing your basic pitch? Do you see new ways to approach your network, prospects, media, investors, etc.? If so, what are your next steps? How will you implement the lessons and teachings in this book? I have not done my job if you haven't looked at your pitch(es) and see room for improvement. I have not done my job if you have not looked at your network and networking groups and see you have been in a comfort zone that no longer serves you. What other areas can you improve? Is your social media content due for an evaluation and elevation? How are you engaging your potential referrals or affiliate partners? Start working on this now! Do not read forward, and do not pass go until you do. Make it a team effort. Ask others for help, possibly a trusted advisor. Before I conclude this chapter, I would be remiss if I did not ask you to consider some of these ingenious ways to make sure you have created your own lane in your industry.

> - What are you CURRENTLY known for?
> - Do you have a tagline that is easy for you to recite and for others to remember?
> - Ask your network to tell you what they know you for as a speaker and/or entrepreneur?
> - Does how you present yourself measure up to how your network sees you? If not, is the way your network sees you greater than how you present yourself? Ask for more feedback from your network.
> - How are you booking speaking gigs? Is it working for you, or are you still on empty?
> - What do you plan to do differently to get companies or other prospects to pay you attention?
> - Have you started blogging, podcasting, or doing Facebook and/or LinkedIn Lives?
> - How are you sharing your authentic self with others?
> - Ask your network who they think are your biggest competitors and why.
> - Do you consider their opinions in line with yours as far as your competitors?
> - Is self-doubt creeping in and making its presence known? How can you change this narrative? Do you practice reciting affirmations? Do you have a strong support network?

> Do you back away from what you need to do for fear nothing will work out? If so, I challenge you to consider all the good things that could occur if it does work out. Change your mindset starting today!

Your next opportunity is staring right at you. Never go to an event, a cause, or a virtual training without being ready to showcase your craft. Always volunteer to answer questions. Be prepared to pitch yourself at all times. You have no idea who is already in the room. So, make it great!

The BIG ASK

Now that we are almost at the end of this book, let me share some #truetea with you. I, too, have been afraid to try new things. I have squandered many opportunities because I thought I did not deserve it or was not good enough. I have had times when I let society shape my opinions of myself and others. I have even let other people's opinions color how I see myself and other people operating in their zone of genius. I have been jealous of those who are winning while I was in my never-ending losing season. Where did that get me? Absolutely nowhere!

You see, to truly be a Bad Bitch, you MUST realize you are the one calling the shots in your life. No one else. Without taking action or even questioning your assumptions, you will NEVER grow to the heights you have seen in your vision. Seek to challenge yourself daily, even when it is not convenient or fun. Seek to inspire yourself to rise above average, random, or ordinary. If most of society thinks one way, why is it that the greats do something totally different? Have you ever noticed that to achieve greatness, you have to avoid believing what others say is impossible? You MUST believe in the impossible and improbable. Do not allow group thinking to stunt your growth. Break free of society's mental and physical chains. There is a reason most people are depressed, bored, and in bad

63

relationships or clinging to relationships that no longer serve them. They settle for what is comfortable and familiar, and they honestly believe deep in their heart that nothing will ever get better.

In the spirit of truth, making A BIG ASK is critical to your business starting, growing, and thriving. From the beginning, I want you to have the #RockStarConfidence and courage to do so. Most people do not have their true needs, wants, and desires because they never asked to have them all met. From this day forward, I want you to commit to making A BIG ASK every day. Flex those courage muscles. Trust me, men do this every day with women, jobs, or anything else they want and need. Is there shame in this? I say no. We all have needs, wants, and desires that we would like to have met. So, what are you waiting for? Need some help and guidance? The #KillerPitchMaster is glad you asked for my assistance. Here are some REAL-WORLD POINTERS from the trenches!

COACHING CORNER: #TRUETEA
ON GETTING WHAT YOU WANT NOW

➢ **Clarity is essential.** Can you clearly articulate what you need, want, and desire for your business or speaking career at a moment's notice? Or are you still being vague, hoping people will understand? NEWSFLASH! THEY WON'T. Clarity is important for both sides to know what you need and how they can be instrumental in helping.

➢ **What is the purpose of your need, want, or desire?** This pertains to your endgame. If you received what you requested, how does this contribute to your bottom line? Are you moving the needle forward? It is important to know the purpose for whatever you are asking to receive, and with clarity, you will shake up the game all around you.

➤ **A specific approach for different audiences.** You will not always be in the same room with the same people. Therefore, it is best to try different pitch and speaking approaches. How does this help? As you learn to read other's body language, you will be able to craft a "killer" pitch that will set you "head and shoulders" above everyone else. Knowing how to be a chameleon and adapt is one of the greatest lessons to learn in your career, business, and life. Play the game to win BIG, not barely. People should be shocked and left in awe when you open your mouth and establish clearly and convincingly who you are and what you uniquely bring to the table.

➤ **The closeness of the relationship determines how far to push or persist.** For the person you make the BIG ASK of, have you established enough of a relationship for what you are requesting? In some ways, this matters, and in other ways, it does not. I have secured my biggest deals and contracts with those who are not close, but I traded on the mystique and other people's positive referrals. For those who are super close to you, let down your guard. Be real and transparent with them. Take into account that people don't want to be sold to, but they love to buy. Also, being associated with a winner like you may open doors for them in the future.

➤ **Make the BIG ASK more than just your needs.** ASK for above and beyond. This is a great lesson to learn. Most of us have been conditioned only to seek the bare minimum of what we need. I say fuck that! If you listen to men and, more importantly, influential people, they start high and negotiate down. Are people shocked by their audacity? Hell yeah, but you also engender respect. Does this always work? No, but imagine how often it does. The truth is you have to have the courage to ask for more than you need and want. The more you do it, the easier it gets! Remember, game respects game. If you do not bring your A-game and ask (and sometimes demand your worth), others will view you as weak. Don't let this be you.

➢ **Prepare for Objections.** Sometimes you win; sometimes you lose. In every negotiation, there may be sticking points. Some may challenge your prices, your assumptions, your speaking fees, etc. It happens every day, so that's why you prepare in advance. Anticipate the most common objections, and as they continue to come up, adjust your pitch accordingly. Leave nothing to chance and keep a poker face. Play the game!

What Is Your
Power Pitch Skillset?

Many times, we are our own worst enemy! Am I right? We believe the lies others pour into us and then wonder why our growth has paused. That is why it's important to guard your heart and mind. See yourself clearly as you are without the judgment of others. Do you like yourself? Are you growing to love yourself? Do you see yourself through the eyes of others' standards or your own? What would it take for you to leave your comfort zone and existing networks to go BIG? (Whatever that means to you.)

Next, I want you, right here and right now, to make a BOLD and UNAPOLOGETIC decision that it's worth fighting for your dreams. That means you will take ACTION NOW! Not now, but RAHT NOW (as my granddaddy would say). Commit fully to this journey of entrepreneurship and/or speaking. Do what you MUST do daily. As Doreen Rainey says, "Success is a habit and must be paid for in advance!" Therefore, you must make this BOLD and UNAPOLOGETIC decision to focus on what truly matters to you. You cannot live your life in others' thoughts and opinions. GOD gave you a vision, and I promise HE needs NO co-signers.

So, before we depart, allow me to offer you some "Bitch Playbook Philosophies" and what it truly means to own your power pitch skillset. What is the Power Pitch Skillset? Do you remember the 7 Branding Bitches from my first book? Well, here they are again! Yes, their same individual personalities and characteristics will help propel you to embrace who you are! Let's take a dance through history with these amazing women, shall we?

➢ **Unstoppable Bitch** ~ The woman who has lost so much and sacrificed it all, that she can ONLY win. She is the woman that has to prove that she is the best of the best. The one that can't stop no matter how bad circumstances are!

➢ **Power Bitch** ~ By her confidence and cunning alone, she simply owns the room and bends others to her will. Her legacy remains long after she leaves the room.

➢ **Flawed Bitch** ~ The one that everybody doubts but has a right seat at the table. She is fighting against society, culture, and everything else that tells her that she looks and acts wrong. Yet, she shows up, defies everything and her excellence cannot be denied.

➢ **Funny Bitch** ~ Injects humor into everything. She is fun, refreshing, and full of life. She draws you in by her excitement and passion.

➢ **Mysterious Bitch** ~ The woman that no one can figure out. What you think or assume is often times never true about her. She creates her own standards in silence and keeps others guessing.

➤ **Creative Bitch** ~ She is the ultimate performer that uses her environment to tell and sell her story.

➤ **Numbers Bitch** ~ The money bitch hands down. Numbers always tell her a story and she can decipher it pretty well. She is a true financial genius and guru.

Now that you have connected to your inner bad bitch, answer some real questions to understand your skillset:

How do you feel about your pitch right now?

_____

_____

_____

_____

_____

_____

Have you taken the Bad Bitches Quiz? What are your results? https://pitchingforprofit.com/

_____

_____

_____

_____

_____

_____

_____

_____

_____

_____

_____

_____

_____

_____

Were you surprised by the results?

_____

_____

_____

_____

What do you need to do differently now?

_____

_____

_____

_____

_____

_____

_____

_____

_____

What noises and voices do you need to get out of your head about going full force in pitching?

_____

_____

_____

_____

_____

_____

_____

_____

_____

_____

Whose life are you living? Yours or someone else's?

_____

_____

_____

_____

_____

_____

_____

_____

_____

_____

Precious L. Williams

Do you know how to create a basic pitch?

_____

_____

_____

_____

Do you know how to create a "killer" pitch?

_____

_____

_____

_____

Which industry are you in?

_____

_____

_____

_____

Who is "killing it" as a speaker or entrepreneur in your industry?

_____

_____

_____

_____

_____

What is your specific niche in your industry?

_____

_____

_____

_____

What do you do better than anyone else hands down?

_____

_____

_____

_____

Do you have testimonials and facts attesting to your strengths and gifts?

_____

_____

_____

_____

_____

_____

_____

_____

Precious L. Williams

Who is your target market? Why?

_____

_____

_____

_____

_____

_____

_____

_____

_____

Are you thinking BIG enough or too small?

_____

_____

_____

_____

_____

_____

_____

_____

_____

_____

What products or services do you have in your Bad Bitches Playbook arsenal? List them below.

_____

_____

_____

_____

_____

_____

_____

_____

_____

_____

_____

_____

_____

_____

_____

_____

_____

_____

_____

_____

_____

_____

NOW WE ARE HERE...

HerStory

Who is Precious L. Williams? I have worked with Microsoft, LinkedIn, Google, NBC Universal, Fortune 500 executives, speakers, and entrepreneurs. Also, I have been featured on *Shark Tank, CNN, WSJ,* and in *Forbes Magazine, Black Enterprise Magazine, Essence Magazine,* and the movie *LEAP.* I am a 13-time national elevator pitch champion and the proud founder and CEO of Perfect Pitches by Precious.

If we pull the curtains back a few short years ago, you will learn that this hasn't always been my story, though. I almost lost it all, in more ways than one. Experiencing Imposter Syndrome, not believing enough in my talent and abilities, and having a mindset based on past failures caused me almost not to see the successes I experience today.

Why does any of this matter to you? Why SHOULD it matter? Because no matter what your age, I NEED you to know that you are talented, beautiful, and playing way too small. I

NEED you to know that I overcame a severe alcohol addiction, lost the love of my life, and was in toxic relationships. Imagine how much further I would be if I had not gone through those trials and tribulations. My hope is that you can avoid these things happening to you.

I know I'm supposed to list my achievements in this section. Well, my greatest accomplishments are being my grandparents' "golden" child and inspiring young girls as well as grown women to bet everything on themselves, daring them to DREAM BIG and WIN. The vision you hold in your mind's eye will not die unless you kill it.

I created the *Bad Bitches and Power Pitches* series to uplift women of all ages to let you know that contrary to what society says, your best is yet to come! Believe in the beauty and future of your dreams.

Since I was five years old, I have known that I was destined for a life in front of the camera. Even at age forty-one, I still know this. Have I given up? NEVER! The older I get, the more I see time as a precious gift. I now see my mistakes with more clarity and grace. I see the failures I have had as stepping-stones to success. I am amazed at how my body functions and how the fresh air in the morning smells. I love hugs more now than ever and understand what true love is despite the world's darkness. I appreciate the little things that I once took for granted.

Tomorrow is not promised to any of us. So, start working on making your dreams a reality right now! This means making connections that matter. Start changing your networks to ones that serve you, your business, career, and life goals. Make the BIG ASK NOW! Keep it moving and know that not every no means never. Sometimes the timing is not right. There will come a time when the yesses will come fast and furious.

My greatest joy come from seeing women succeed, especially as we get older. Society likes to make the older generation feel like they are no longer valuable. My take is that our experiences make us invaluable to the next generation. Stand in the power of who you have become—beholden to no one but GOD. With clarity comes the peace of making peace with the past. The good, the bad, and the ugly of it all led you to this moment where faith and hope become action, and you will see the true beauty and magic reflected in who you are NOW.

I am right where I am supposed to be. Years ago, I looked down on those less fortunate than me—the addicts, the homeless, those who were truly suffering. GOD wanted to humble me and show me that in the blink of an eye, that could become my fate. I battled back from a severe alcohol addiction that threatened my very life. I became homeless, and it colored every aspect of my world. Friends came and went; toxic people were removed from my life. Today, I count it all joy. The bad things I went through made me much stronger. Everything I used to be mad at GOD about, I bless HIS holy name for now.

Sometimes you have to lose it all to win again. When everything is taken from you, you gain a different perspective of looking at things—not through the eyes of lack but from the eyes of seeing what truly matters most. It is a gift. A gift that keeps on giving. I am much more loving and kind to my fellow man. I look at others through the eyes of GOD. Not pity, not charity but from a sincere place of seeing the good in others and knowing that our circumstances are not who we are. Circumstances are what we go through on this journey called life. Me being stronger and wiser is the gift of age and time. Thank GOD!

My wish is that this book puts your fear, doubt, and worries to rest. You are equipped for battle and to WIN BIG! Let me leave you with this:

Prepare to take MASSIVE and small actions daily to reach the destination you have set for yourself and your business. That vision you have had since a child, prepare for its birth. Prepare for the joys and pain. Nothing worth having comes

Precious L. Williams

easy, but what makes this easier to bear is that when you achieve it, you flex new muscles and will be able to tackle anything that comes your way. The greatest to have ever done it faced the same things. They confronted their demons. They faced the doubt and fear within. They fought till the great, not bitter, end. You are a fighter and fighters fight!

Let's get it, my Bad Bitches! Are you ready? The #KillerPitchMaster is right here with you, holding your hand, challenging you, and prepping you. You are not alone. GOD has you, and He sent me so you could witness a trailblazer do it with vision, passion, and determination.

I love you!

Precious L. Williams

STAY CONNECTED

Website:
https://www.perfectpitchesbyprecious.com/

Online/Digital Courses:
https://www.perfectpitchesbyprecious.com/store/Online-Training-c49499162

Products and Services:
https://www.perfectpitchesbyprecious.com/store/

MORE BOOKS BY PRECIOUS

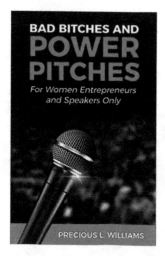

Warning! What you're about to read is a step-by-step guide to winning at the game of life. The stakes are high. So, read this only if you dare. Have you ever wondered what some women entrepreneurs and speakers do to stand out and have prospects, the media, and investors seeking them out? What's their secret sauce? How did they transcend from being average to becoming extraordinary?

My dear, they are bad bitches with power pitches! A serial entrepreneur, international professional speaker, and 13-time elevator pitch champion, #KillerPitchMaster Precious Williams shows you how despite growing up in poverty & she took the business, television, and media worlds by storm through the power of being a bad bitch. In her greatness, you will see yourself and learn how to unleash your bad bitch. She also shares the seven types of specific-branding bad bitches. Through Precious's experiences, she will help you discover or resurrect the bad bitch inside of you.

Bad Bitches with Power Pitches provides the tools of success that will have prospects seeking you out, event planners booking you for speaking engagements, and the media clamoring to get the inside scoop on you. Wherever you are in your entrepreneurial journey, this no-holds-barred, no-nonsense book will show you how to utilize your bad-bitch mentality to achieve your dreams. Dare greatly!

Precious L. Williams steps up her game in her follow-up to her best-seller, *Bad Bitches and Power Pitches: For Women Entrepreneurs and Speakers Only*. Ms. Williams' second offering gets you ready for the boardroom, the stage, media and/or investors, by teaching everything from pitching to the ingenious tips, tricks, and techniques for any woman who is ready to dominate her industry. Ready to make a name for yourself, dominate the competition and stand out online and offline, this workbook is for you!

The Bad Bitches and Power Pitches Workbook is a perfect addition for the entrepreneur and/or speaker who is ready to break all boundaries and surpass that glass ceiling!

All Precious' Books are Available Now on Amazon...and so on and her website!

CPSIA information can be obtained
at www.ICGtesting.com
Printed in the USA
FSHW020732310321

9 781736 611821